I0163076

You Are
FORGIVEN

31 PROMISES FROM THE HOLY SCRIPTURES

Moments to Remind You of God's Forgiveness

Merle M. Mills

© 2013 by Merle M. Mills

Printed in the United States of America

All rights reserved. No part of this publication may be reproduced, stored in a retrieval system, or transmitted in any form or by any means—for example, electronic, photocopy, recording—without the prior written permission of the publisher. The only exception is brief quotations.

ISBN-13:978-0-9886 162-1-9

Scripture quotations noted KJV are taken from the Holy Bible, King James Version ®, KJV

Scripture quotations noted NLT are taken from the Holy Bible, New Living Translation, copyright © 1996, 2004. Used by permission of Tyndale House Publishers, Inc., Wheaton, Illinois 60189. All rights reserved.

www.changedthrutheword.org
www.nomoreasecret.blogspot.com

Interior Design by Evelyn J. Wagoner

Acknowledgements

To my God,
thank You for forgiving me.
As long as You give me breath,
I will serve You.

To my family,
thank you for supporting me
by giving me the freedom of many hours
at my computer.

To those who generously support me,
share your God-given talents with me,
pray for me, and who wish to remain anonymous,
may God bless you much more abundantly.

Introduction

One definition given by Webster's Dictionary for the word *forgive* is TO PARDON. In Scriptures the word is also interpreted TO PARDON.

Most of us have done things we would like to be pardoned for. Scripture tells us in 1 John 1:9: **"But if we confess our sins to Him, He is faithful and just to forgive us our sins and to cleanse us from all wickedness."**

Have you committed a sin that you would like God's pardon for?

I have chosen 31 Scriptural references that have helped me and will remind you of God's extravagant forgiveness after sin. These verses will be valuable tools for daily study, memorization **("I have hidden Your word in my heart, that I might not sin against You."** Psalm 119:11) and meditation.

My prayer is that, as you read these promises, you will join me in receiving them. You will see, as I have seen, your life transformed from pain to peace ... sadness to joy ... weakness to strength.

May God bless you as you understand ... you are forgiven.

Merle M. Mills

Contents

Promise
ONE

**I have swept away your sins like a cloud.
I have scattered your offenses like the
morning mist. Oh, return to Me, for I have
paid the price to set you free.**
(Isaiah 44:22)

When we sin, we offend God, ourselves, and others. The good news is that God sent His only Son Jesus Christ who paid the price to set us free from our offenses and wrongdoings.

What have you done to offend God, yourself, or others?

Today, our God is waiting with open arms for you to receive His great gift of freedom, love, and forgiveness.

Read and Memorize

Romans 5:8; Luke 4:18-19; Psalm 63:3

Promise
TWO

**He is so rich in kindness and grace that
He purchased our freedom with the blood
of His Son and forgave our sins.**
(Ephesians 1:7)

When we make the decision to accept God's gift of forgiveness, questions will immediately fill our minds. Questions such as: Do you know what you have done? How could God forgive you?

Stand firm, believe, and accept God's Word: **"I am the Lord, I change not."**[1] **"Heaven and earth shall pass away but My Word shall not pass away."**[2]

Jesus Christ—the same yesterday, today, and forever.[3] **The grass withers and the flowers fade, but the Word of our God stands forever.**[4]

References:

[1]Malachi 3:6; [2]Matthew 24:35;
[3]Hebrews 13:8; [4]Isaiah 40:8

Promise
THREE

For He has rescued us from the kingdom of darkness and transferred us into the Kingdom of His dear Son, who purchased our freedom and forgave our sins.
(Colossians 1:13-14)

Some of my most frightening moments as a child were when we experienced a power failure and darkness filled our home. Until my mom or dad lit a candle, my brothers, sisters, and I would huddle together in fear of the dark. The entrance of that spark of light would bring smiles to our little faces.

Our Heavenly father has done the same in our lives. He has rescued us from Satan's kingdom of darkness into the Kingdom of light. Does this promise bring a smile to your face?

Read and Memorize

John 8:31-31; Isaiah 58:6; Psalm 116:8;
1 John 1:5

Promise

FOUR

**You forgave the guilt of Your people--yes,
You covered all their sins.**
(Psalm 85:2)

During one of Billy Graham's London Crusades, a psychiatrist said that, in his opinion, 70 percent of those in mental institutions could be immediately discharged if they could find release from their tormenting guilt.[1]

Are you tormented by your past sin? Let this promise saturate your mind. Remind yourself daily that forgiveness is yours for the asking.

[1] *How to Handle a Bad Conscience* (Ray Steadman)

Read and Memorize

Philippians 4:8; Isaiah 26:3; Psalm 25:5

Promise
FIVE

He has removed our sins as far from us as the east is from the west.
(Psalm 103:12)

One definition of the word *remove* is TO PUSH ASIDE. A line from the song *"East to West"* by Casting Crowns says, *"'cause You know just how far the east is from the west."*

This promise is for you and for me. Our God promises *to push aside* our sins and, since only He knows how far the east is from the west, we can rest assured they are far from us.

Read and Memorize

John 6:37; Psalm 107:1; Revelation 3:20

Promise
SIX

***"Come now, let's settle this," says the LORD.
"Though your sins are like scarlet,
I will make them as white as snow.
Though they are red like crimson,
I will make them as white as wool."***
(Isaiah 1:18)

All our successes, achievements or accomplishments will never exceed the feeling of knowing the freedom and forgiveness promised by the Great Forgiver—Jesus Christ.

Remember what you have done. Ask God for forgiveness. Next, move into your future knowing and believing that you are forgiven and that He has promised to exchange scarlet sins and make them white as snow, crimson sins and make them white as wool.

Read and Memorize

John 10:10; Philippians 3:13; Jeremiah 29:11

Promise
SEVEN

But You offer forgiveness that we might learn to fear You.
(Psalm 130:4)

In the beginning, God said, "Let there be light," and then created night and day, which continue today. God's Words in this promise offered from the Holy Scriptures have the same power and ability today as they did when first written.

Does forgiveness sound too good to be true? Of course it does. As we watch night and day exchange daily, let it be a reminder of the hope of being loved and forgiven by a God whose Word is changeless and Who forgives unconditionally.

Read and Memorize

Genesis 1:3-5; Isaiah 54:8; Colossians 1:21

Promise
EIGHT

He forgives all my sins
and heals all my diseases.
(Psalm 103:3)

In his book, *Psalms for Today*, Peter Wallace wrote:

"God's forgiveness of us knows no boundaries ... your sins have been removed. You need not live under their burden. If you are struggling with guilt over the sins that have plagued you in the past, it's time to let go. If you need to work through them, seek help. If a pattern of sin still exists in your life, seek help. But don't forget this truth: You are forgiven. God accepts you totally and loves you completely."

Read and Memorize

Philippians 3:13; Psalm 126:5; Matthew 11:28

Promise
NINE

I—yes, I alone—will blot out your sins for My own sake and will never think of them again.
(Isaiah 43:25)

Does God have a memory problem? Certainly not! He *chooses* not to remind us of our sin. We have the choice to repent, ask for forgiveness, accept it, believe, and choose to live the abundant life He has promised us.

Read and Memorize

John 10:10; Numbers 6:24; Luke 12:32

Promise

TEN

And I will forgive their wickedness,
and I will never again remember their sins.
(Hebrews 8:12)

According to Sandy MacGregor, our subconscious mind *"has the ability to record and remember every incident that it experiences."* [1] This may be one of the reasons why sometimes we have difficulty forgetting our sin.

Today's promise reminds us that God chooses not to remember our past sin. It is vital to spend time every day reading what God says about loving and forgiving us so that our subconscious mind will overflow with memories of hope and acceptance.

[1]studentstepstosuccess.com/index.php

Read and Memorize

Lamentations 3:22-23; Psalms 59:16; Psalm 108:4;
John 15:13; Jeremiah 29:11

Promise
ELEVEN

***O Lord, You are so good, so ready
to forgive, so full of unfailing love for all
who ask for Your help.***
(Psalm 86:5)

In our relationships, if we wrong one another, we may sometimes think twice before asking for forgiveness from that person. We may think we'll be rejected or that our apology will not be accepted.

Unlike human nature, our God waits for us to repent and ask for forgiveness. He is ready to forgive us without rejection; ready to respond in love when we ask for His help; ready to accept us and completely restore us to an uninterrupted relationship.

Read and Memorize

James 4:8; John 6:37; Psalms 78:39

Promise
TWELVE

Where is another God like You,
who pardons the guilt of the remnant,
overlooking the sins of His special people?
You will not stay angry with Your
people forever, because You delight
in showing unfailing love.
(Micah 7:18)

One definition of *sin* in Webster's Dictionary is the BREAKING OF A LAW OF GOD. David the Psalmist wrote in Psalm 51, **"Against You and You alone have I sinned ... because of Your great compassion ... wash me clean from my guilt. Purify me from my sin."**

God answered David's prayer, and this example continues to demonstrate God's willingness to forgive us, to not stay angry with us, and to show us His unfailing love.

Read and Memorize

Psalms 86:10; Ephesians 2:4;
Lamentations 3:22-23

15

THIRTEEN

***You have in love to my soul
delivered it from the pit of corruption:
for You have cast all my sins
behind Your back.***
(Isaiah 38:17b) [KJV]

Our God's desire to forgive our sin is preceded by His great love for us. Our enemy Satan wants us to remember our sin, so we can continue to live feeling condemned and unworthy. To the reverse, our God wants to set us free from guilt, condemnation, and regret, so we can share the good news of His unlimited forgiveness with friends ... co-workers ... children ... family members.

This unlimited forgiveness has cast all our sins behind God's back. When we accept this promise, it has the power to cleanse us and give us a brand new start.

Read and Memorize

Isaiah 43:18; Luke 8:39; Psalm 119:46

FOURTEEN

Then Jesus said to the woman,
"Your sins are forgiven."
(Luke 7:48)

When we know our God has forgiven us, has pardoned and saved us from the consequential punishment of sin, it will make a difference in our lives. How? We will walk with confidence. We will speak with confidence. Our sleep will be different. Why? Because the burden of the shame, the feelings of regret and guilt will no longer haunt our minds.

Do not move to the next page until you settle it once and for all. Will you let this be your prayer?
"I will accept God's gift of forgiveness. I will celebrate my freedom from shame, regret, and guilt. Thank You, Heavenly Father, for loving me, for accepting me, and for forgiving me."

Read and Memorize

Romans 9:33; Isaiah 61:7; Psalms 31:1

Promise
FIFTEEN

**Jesus gave His life for our sins,
just as God our Father planned,
in order to rescue us from this evil
world in which we live.**
(Galatians 1:4)

One definition of the word *rescue* is TO FREE FROM CONFINEMENT, DANGER, OR EVIL. In March 2012, the world witnessed the story of Stephanie Decker who selflessly lost her legs saving the lives of her two children from the danger and evil of a monster tornado in Marysville, Indiana.

Today, the whole world can still witness and partake in the selfless act of the One, Jesus Christ, who gave His life in order to set us free from the danger and evil of sin.

Read and Memorize

1 John 3:16; Psalms 86:13; Colossians 1:13

Promise
SIXTEEN

For God so loved the world, that He gave His only begotten Son, that whosoever believeth in Him should not perish, but have everlasting life.
(John 3:16 KJV)

God's promise to forgive us is based on His unconditional love for us. In his book, *Unto the Hills,* Billy Graham wrote, *"The reason God hates sin is that it is sin which, left unforgiven, sends men and women out into a timeless eternity in hell. God is not willing that any should perish, but that all might come to a knowledge of Him."*

This promise outlines the reason Jesus gave His life, to set us free from sin and to give us a hope for the future. Wouldn't you say that is a demonstration of His extravagant and unlimited love?

Read and Memorize

1 John 3:8; Psalm 139:8; John 15:13

SEVENTEEN

**The payment for sin is death,
but the gift that God freely gives
is everlasting life found in
Christ Jesus our Lord.**
(Romans 6:23) [GWT]

Sin is defined as WRONGDOING; AN ACT CONTRARY TO THE WILL AND LAW OF GOD and, in God's sight, deserving of death. Instead, His great love for us promises a gift. This gift takes us from wrongdoing to doing good … from breaking His law to desiring to keep that law … from death to everlasting life.

A gift is something to be received. I have never refused a gift and certainly would not refuse this one. Would you?

Read and Memorize

John 15:16; Psalm 48:14; Joshua 1:8

Promise
EIGHTEEN

And I am convinced that nothing can ever separate us from God's love. Neither death nor life, neither angels nor demons, neither our fears for today nor our worries about tomorrow--not even the powers of hell can separate us from God's love. No power in the sky above or in the earth below--indeed, nothing in all creation will ever be able to separate us from the love of God that is revealed in Christ Jesus our Lord.
(Romans 8:38-39)

Nothing we have done can ever separate us from God's love. Asking for God's forgiveness will cover any wrong that we have done. This is possible through the power in the sacrifice that was made on the cross by Christ Jesus our Savior. The offer of forgiveness is always available. Will you accept it today?

Heavenly Father, for the wrong that I have done, forgive me. Thank You for receiving me into Your love. In Jesus' name, amen.

NINETEEN

**For I will forgive their iniquity,
and I will remember their sin no more.**
(Jeremiah 31:34c KJV)

I cannot explain what happens when I press the 'on' switch on my computer, or the 'on' switch on the lamp next to it. I just know that, together, they allow me the benefit of many productive and rewarding hours of reading, researching, and writing.

Neither can I explain what happens in my soul when I daily open the pages of the Holy Scriptures and read promises such as this about my Heavenly Father's offer of forgiveness. The words of Isaac Newton in the beloved hymn, *When I Survey the Wondrous Cross*, say it well:

> *Were the whole realm of nature mine,*
> *That were an offering far too small;*
> *Love so amazing, so divine,*
> *Demands my soul, my life, my all.*

Read and Memorize

Psalm 116:12; Philippians 3:10; Galatians 2:20

Promise
TWENTY

All glory to Him who loves us and has freed us from our sins by shedding His blood for us.
(Revelation 1:5b)

Jesus fulfilled the requirement of the shedding of blood for sin once yearly as set out in the Old Testament (Exodus 30:10; Numbers 15:27) by becoming the sacrifice once and forever (Hebrews 10:12). Without the shedding of blood there is no forgiveness or pardon of sins (Hebrews 9:22; Leviticus 17:11). Jesus demonstrated His great love for us by giving His life and shedding His blood to set us free, releasing us from the bondage of sin. Do I understand this totally?

Before traveling by air, do you step into the cockpit and ask the crew to show you their credentials? Most people don't. We simply trust that the pilot is trained and capable of taking us to our destination.

By faith, I have trusted the Word of the living God, and it has taken me to a destination of peace, joy, and strength. I guarantee it will do the same for you.

Read and Memorize

Romans 5:7-8; Hebrews 11:1; Psalm 71:1;
Proverbs 3:5-6; Psalm 13:5

Promise
TWENTY-ONE

**For God did not send His Son
into the world to condemn the world,
but to save the world through Him.**
(John 3:17 NIV)

God created man with a conscience. Dr. Timothy Lin, PhD, describes it as, *"conscience is the faculty of man's knowing right and wrong in connection with laws made known to him/her. When our emotions and mental faculties relax after completing an action, conscience either crowns us with satisfaction, happiness, and courage for what we have done or summons us to the bar of justice where she thunders judgment, which gives us a bad or guilty conscience."*

Committing sin and breaking the law of God deserves condemnation. Our God promises that if we confess our sin, He will save us and ***"crown us with satisfaction."***

Thank You, Heavenly Father, for not condemning me, but for saving me from sin. In Jesus' Name, amen.

Read and Memorize

Philippians 2:5; Deuteronomy 30:19;
Romans 8:1; Hebrews 10:22

TWENTY-TWO

***Finally, I confessed all my sins to You
and stopped trying to hide my guilt.
I said to myself, "I will confess my rebellion
to the LORD." And You forgave me!
All my guilt is gone.***
(Psalm 32:5)

Whether we consider the sin major or minor, small or large, it produces guilt. David the Psalmist experienced this guilt. His only relief was openly confessing his sin to our Heavenly Father who, in turn, forgave him.

Is there some sin you have committed that you feel cannot be forgiven? I joined the Psalmist, ***"confessed my rebellion to the Lord,"*** and He forgave me. Now I live with a grateful heart asking Him every day to help me not to sin.

This promise of forgiveness has the ability to do the same for you.

Read and Memorize

Psalm 66:18; Psalm 51:3-4;
Romans 6:18; Galatians 5:1

Promise
TWENTY-THREE

***But You are a God of forgiveness, gracious
and merciful, slow to become angry, and rich
in unfailing love. You did not abandon them.***
(Nehemiah 9:17b)

Trust plays an important factor in believing what
someone will do. I believe one of the main reasons
we entertain the voice of doubt after asking for
forgiveness is that we do not fully trust God. One
definition of the word trust is *"to have confidence
in."* How do we develop confidence to know that
God will forgive us? By reading His Word ... by
memorizing His Word ... by speaking His Word.

As we read the Bible daily, we begin to have more
and more confidence about who He is, about what
He says, and about what He will do. Then only will
we understand that He is gracious, merciful,
compassionate, and slow to become angry with us.
He does not abandon us, but draws us to Himself
with His rich unfailing love.

Read and Memorize

Galatians 1:4; Psalm 136:1; Psalm 145:8;
Isaiah 54:10; Ephesians 3:19

Promise
TWENTY-FOUR

Be encouraged, My child!
Your sins are forgiven.
(Matthew 9:2)

No matter what sin from the past comes to mind or hinders us from living God's promised abundant life (John 10:10), God has the power to forgive. Is it a lifestyle issue? Is it a personal issue? Is it a past abortion? Is it something you have kept secret for years? The guilt, the shame, the anger, the depression, the regret you have told no one about, His power can forgive it today.

As Oswald Chambers states in his book, *My Utmost For His Highest, "God forgives sin only because of the death of Christ … conviction is given to us as a gift from God. Jesus Christ hates the sin in people, and Calvary is the message of His hatred."*

Come. Leave it at Calvary today. Walk away forgiven and loved by the Master.

Read and Memorize

Galatians 1:4; 2 Corinthians 5:17;
Psalm 119:92; John 11:50

TWENTY-FIVE

Yes, turn to our God,
for He will forgive generously.
(Isaiah 55:7c)

Just imagine! The God who you and I have sinned against asking us to turn to Him and He will forgive us generously? This promise makes me not want to do wrong or to break any of His laws. Our God does not wait for us to clean ourselves up before we come to Him. When we turn to Him, He accepts us just as we are and He does the miraculous work of cleaning us up and forgiving us generously.

Read and Memorize

Psalm 145:8; Luke 15: 21-24; Jeremiah 31:3

TWENTY-SIX

***Though we are overwhelmed by our sins,
You forgive them all.***
(Psalm 65:3)

The burden of sin can be overwhelming. I may be overwhelmed by my sins, but my God is not. Are you overwhelmed by the burden of sin? You and I are so important to God that He has promised to forgive them ALL.

Read and Memorize

Psalm 61:2; Job 42:1; 1 Peter 5:7

TWENTY-SEVEN

I will cleanse them of their sins against me and forgive all their sins of rebellion.
(Jeremiah 33:8)

Recently a visiting pastor shared a significant message at my church. He talked about how many of us have an untold story that we would share with no one. The good news, though, was that our Heavenly Father has answers for these untold stories with the told stories of what He has done.

This is how I immediately saw myself in this equation:

MY UNTOLD STORY = GUILT + SHAME + REGRET

HIS TOLD STORY = FREEDOM[1] + PEACE[2] + FORGIVENESS[3]

"Father, I give you my untold story, and I never want it again, In Jesus name, amen!"

Do you have an untold story? Will you make this great exchange today?

References

[1]Ephesians 1:7; [2]Colossians 1:14; [3]Daniel 9:9

TWENTY-EIGHT

**But the Lord our God is merciful
and forgiving, even though we have
rebelled against Him.**
(Daniel 9:9)

God created us and placed the power in us to live holy, pure, and blameless before Him. When we sin, it is considered rebellion. Conscious or unconscious sin hinders our relationship with our Heavenly Father. I urge you, if and when you sin, go to God immediately, confess the sin, and ask for forgiveness. He promises to be merciful and to forgive.

Heavenly Father, may I never abuse Your generous offer of forgiveness as an excuse to sin. Help me to be pure, holy, and blameless before You each moment of each day that I may overcome the rebellion of sin. In Jesus' name, amen.

Read and Memorize

Psalm 139:23-24; 1 Peter 1:16;
Leviticus 20:26; Matthew 5:48

Promise
TWENTY-NINE

And forgive us our sins, as we have forgiven those who sin against us.
(Matthew 6:12)

There are times when we will have to extend the same forgiveness that we have received to someone who has wronged us. Jesus though mistreated, wrongly accused, misunderstood, denied, mocked, and betrayed, spoke these words while being crucified***: "Father, forgive them for they don't know what they are doing."***

No, it may not be easy, but, as Lewis B. Smedes said: "*To forgive is to set a prisoner free and discover that the prisoner was you.*"

Read and Memorize

Matthew 6:15; Luke 6:37;
Ephesians 4:32; Leviticus 19:18

Promise
THIRTY

**Once again You will have compassion on us.
You will trample our sins under Your feet and
throw them into the depths of the ocean!**
(Micah 7:19)

In his book, *"The Wonders of Creation,"* Alfred Rehwinkel wrote, *"... there is enough water in the seas to cover the entire face of the earth with a mile and a half of water ... the average depth of the Pacific Ocean is 14,648 feet; of the Atlantic, 12,880 feet; of the Indian, 13,602 feet; and of the Arctic, 3,965 feet."*

Often, I visit the oceanfront for quiet and relaxing times. I am comforted as I envision my Heavenly Father casting my sins into the **"depths of the ocean,"** and I breathe a prayer:

Father, for Your offer of forgiveness, words are inadequate to thank You. Please look into my heart and see the gratefulness written there. In Jesus' name, amen.

Promise
THIRTY-ONE

And Jesus said unto her, "Neither do I condemn you: go, and sin no more."
(John 8:11b KJV 2000)

Jesus spoke these words of promise over two thousand years ago to the woman caught in the act of adultery. This promise stands true today. Whatever sin, wrongdoing, or law of God that you may have broken, fill in the blank _____. Today, Jesus is the only One who has the power to heal, deliver, set free, and restore, and He's saying these same words to you ... **"Neither do I condemn you; go, and sin no more."**

Read and Memorize

Ephesians 2:14; Psalm 30:11;
Philippians 3:13-14; Mark 5:19

And
NOW...

If, after reading this book, you would like to have a personal relationship with Jesus Christ, the One who promises to offer healing, forgiveness, deliverance, peace, and restoration, following is a prayer you can pray:

Father, You have promised that if I confess my sin, You will forgive me and cleanse me from all the wrong I have done (1 John 1:9). I confess now. Forgive me. Fill me with your Holy Spirit. Take my hand and walk with me for the rest of my life. In Jesus' name, amen.

About
THE AUTHOR

As an author and speaker, Merle M. Mills, founder of *Changed through the Word*, ministers throughout the Hampton Roads area sharing the good news of a changed life through words from the Holy Scriptures.

Her prayer is that her reading and listening audience will allow the power of the ever-living God the freedom to do the same in and through their lives.

Her book, *No More a Secret: A Guide to Healing After Abortion*, and the accompanying CD, *No More a Secret*, bring hope and healing to women, especially those experiencing after-abortion trauma. Her recent booklet, *Hand in Hand with the Master*, a 31-day devotional featuring poetry, Scripture, and words of encouragement to remind us of God's love, has also brought hope to many.

Merle resides with her family in Norfolk, Virginia.

Changed Through the Word
P. O. Box 41293
Norfolk, VA 23541

www.changedthrutheword.org
changedthrutheword@gmail.com
www.nomoreasecret.blogspot.com

www.ingramcontent.com/pod-product-compliance
Lightning Source LLC
Chambersburg PA
CBHW060102050426
42448CB00011B/2585